the good Orgasm *guide*

SIMON &
SCHUSTER

Kate Taylor

This edition first published in Great Britain by
Simon & Schuster UK Ltd, 2002
A Viacom Company

1 3 5 7 9 10 8 6 4 2

Simon & Schuster UK Ltd
Africa House
64-78 Kingsway
London WC2B 6AH

www.simonsays.co.uk

Simon & Schuster Australia Sydney

A CIP catalogue record for this book is available from the
British Library

ISBN 0-7432-3116-3

Produced and designed by Elwin Street Limited
Unit 330, 30 Great Guildford Street
London SE1 OHS

Come Here Often?

Orgasms are like buses – big, noisy and ugly when seen from behind. But, like buses, they are available on every street corner if you just know where and when to stick your hand up.

If you're sceptical about that, you're probably a Type B reader. You see there are two types of people who read sex books: Type As are like my friend Linda – gorgeous, beautiful, amazing in bed and comes at the drop of a trouser. I'm serious. She once experienced an orgasm simply driving over speed bumps (which must have been disconcerting for everyone else on the coach). She just seems to be in touch with her orgasmic side. She would buy this book because orgasms are her hobby.

Type B readers, however, are the rest of the population. Like me, you probably love sex and have had an orgasm. Or maybe you haven't. Doesn't matter. The important bit is that you'd like to have one, or more of them – bigger, better and longer. The sort of toe-curling, brain-blistering climaxes that can scorch your mattress and leave your partner with burst eardrums. Or maybe you'd like different orgasms – exotic ones that start with a G or an A and have only recently been discovered by NASA scientists. Or perhaps, you'd just like to have more orgasms with your partner.

Whichever type you are, honey – and you might be a mix of all of them – you've come to the right place. Before you leave, you'll be a one-woman orgasmatron, capable of giving and receiving orgasms that make your neighbours move house. This is not your average sex book. You will not find namby-pamby paragraphs telling you that your vagina is a 'beautiful rose' or advising you to squat over a hand mirror (I tried that once – all I got was an aversion to shellfish.). Good sex takes practise and concentration, but most of all it requires inside information. In between these covers is everything to make you better in between yours. Tips, tricks and techniques tell you exactly how you can come and often.

So what are you waiting for? Come on girls. Cancel the papers, pull down the blinds and take the phone off the hook. We're going in...

GETTING IN THE MOOD

You've probably already heard that good sex starts in your head. Without guidance, you probably thought that meant something tricky to do with blow-jobs, tutted cynically and gave up. But it doesn't. It means that if you want to become orgasmic physically, you have to think orgasmic mentally.

1

Orgasms can be difficult to achieve. Otherwise, buses would be full of women screaming in delight every time it hit a speedbump. Orgasms require you to let go – give up control, ditch hang-ups, relax completely – which can be almost impossible if you're carrying around a load of mental baggage. This is where we help you dump it.

To be sexy, you have to feel sexy. So, do you? If you do, good for you. I'm sure it shows in your great sex life, your general confidence and your broken bed. But if you don't feel sexy, or if you waver between feeling naughty one minute and neutered the next, don't panic. You're normal.

Why? Upbringing, mostly. We're denied our sex appeal from an early age, and those voices ('Cover your bottom, dear', 'Don't let him go all the way', 'Hands on *top* of the blankets, girls!') stay with us. They're probably still replaying through your brain every time you invite a nice

'Confidence is so sexy. I hate girls who hide their bodies, or point out their bad bits. To be honest, it's only when they point them out that I notice them! A girl who loves herself is always attractive.'

DANIEL, THIRTY-FOUR

TRY THIS NOW!

Want to smell sexy? Then dip your finger into your vagina and dab the moisture behind your ears, like scent. It contains pheromones, and experts believe it can attract the opposite sex.

---

young man in for coffee. Guilt is *rife* in women's brains. And you can't spend half your life trying to be a nice girl, and then expect to jump immediately into full-throttle bad girl mode as soon as the man of your dreams reaches down and touches your thigh.

To release it, don't just ring your Mum and shout at her. Instead, work on believing that you are a sexual person and that you are allowed to have dirty thoughts. It might be as simple as spending time before you go to sleep, accepting those stray thoughts that creep into your brain. Or it might require some expert therapy. Whatever it takes, do it. You have to believe that you *deserve* orgasms. Otherwise your brain will shut off pleasure signals sent up from your body every time.

Boost your sexual confidence

One way of checking your sexual baggage at the bedroom door is just to wait. This is the main reason why women reach their sexual peak in their mid thirties. That's the decade where you finally learn to love yourself, gain confidence in your lovemaking skills, and have shagged enough men to know that sex won't necessarily cause him to run screaming to the hills afterwards. But if you don't fancy waiting, you have to raise your confidence now. We have ways.

I was once told to stand in front of the mirror, naked, and repeat 'You are a beautiful woman', over and over until I finally believed it. Did it help? Did it hell. It was like saying 'I am rich' while reading my overdrawn bank statement. What did help was a boyfriend telling me that almost all naked women are sexy. When it's just you and your lover in the bedroom, he told me, the bloke is not gazing at the girl and thinking 'look at the cellulite on that'. He's thinking, 'Mmmm. Breasts. Bottom. Bits'. He's looking at your naked body and thinking about sex. His IQ is, at that moment, at Forrest Gump levels and he wouldn't care if you had a mutant dwarf growing out of your back. In fact, he would probably like it.

One of the best-selling magazines for men is *Readers Wives*: It features photographs of ordinary women in ordinary bedrooms. It's not glam at all. Because, really, men just like naked ladies. And if you're standing in front of a man, naked, and willing to have sex with him, you are gorgeous.

Of course, if you're with a man who consistently doesn't make you feel gorgeous, ditch him. That's all about his problems, not yours. He feels bad about himself and so wants to make you feel so low you'll be grateful he's around. Healthy? No way. And about as helpful to having orgasms as a barbed-wire G-string.

Another barrier to sexual confidence is feeling dirty, guilty or afraid to let go. The best way of getting over these hang-ups is – and you'll love this – to have loads of sex. I'm serious! (And aren't you pleased?) But sex within relationships. One-night-stands won't help you. They'll make you worse. You need support and love.

Or, it might be that a bad experience has ruined your sexual confidence totally. If that's the case I can only beg you to get professional help. You deserve to feel sexy and orgasmic. It's your birthright as a woman! Don't let anything stand in your way. You're worth it, OK?

'I always hated having sex in front of mirrors because all I could look at was my chunky thighs and bottom. Then my boyfriend told me that I had the sexiest skin — soft, smooth and golden. So that's what I focus on now. I figure if he isn't focusing on my bad bits, why should I?'

TANYA, TWENTY-NINE

'I love it when my wife wears one of my work shirts after we've made love.'

SIMON, THIRTY-THREE

'My lover used to worry that her boobs were too small. She was always hiding them. But as soon as I told her that I loved them — the way they felt, and how hard her nipples got in my mouth — she relaxed. Women shouldn't compare themselves to others. Men don't.'

JOHN, TWENTY-SEVEN

Be sexy every day

The only way to become a sex goddess is to act like one. Start now. Imagine you were the most gorgeous, sexy creature you can imagine. How would you be reading this book? Would you be slumped in an unmade bed, biting your nails, or reclining on a couch sipping Champagne? The phone rings. How do you answer it – hastily, hurriedly, or seductively and optimistically? Picture everything. How you'd dress, where you'd go, what you'd eat, where you'd live.

Then do it! Act 'as if'. Start treating yourself like that sexy vixen who is, at this minute, hiding underneath your baggy jumper or mixed-wash pants. When you act as if you were something, something weird happens to your brain and it actually starts to believe it's true.

I do this every day of my life. In my worst moments I know I'm an average-looking redhead prone to plumpness, with a bum that can look like rice pudding in a bag. But do I act like that? No way! I dress sexily, get regular facials, pamper my body and scrub that lumpy bum every day with steel wool and acid. Everything, in fact, that your regular born-and-bred sex goddess would do. And it works. The most frequent compliment I get is that I'm sexy.

TRY THIS NOW!

Start thinking about sex as often as you can. Remember your last brilliant shag. Relive it. Everything – every noise, sensation and action. Keep that image in your mind all day. You'll give off a glow and you'll feel sexier.

Act 'as if' every chance you get and you will get results. You'll feel good – more confident, more sassy, less prone to eating chocolate in bed – and everyone (including men) will notice. It's not enough just to tell yourself you're sexy, however. You have to walk the walk. Literally. Hip-swinging and slow, with your head high and your heels higher.

Less is more

Want more? OK. Sexiness is composure. Think, 'less is more'. A sexy woman walks slowly, talks quietly and sits still. She looks deep into men's eyes. She doesn't panic or get nervous. She thinks before she acts, and knows her own worth. And throws tights away when they ladder.

How does this help me orgasm?

Beauty tips might look out of place in a book on orgasms. But they're not – all this good stuff is to help you silence that little voice that pipes up, 'Your thighs are fat' just when you could be reaching a climax. Women most often go off sex when their confidence is low – after having a baby, for instance, when they feel fat and tired. Or within a long relationship when the man has stopped complimenting them. Or after a long barren patch of Friday nights at home, alone, eating pizza and watching old romantic movies. To be orgasmic, you have to feel you're worth it. You have to feel desirable. You have to feel rude.

How do I act sexy if I'm single?

Honey, you're in the best position to act sexy. Without a steady partner, the whole world is your dating pool. Do the stuff mentioned above, but also keep thinking that you could meet your perfect partner anywhere, any day. Dress like you'll meet him around the next corner.

Clean hair is sexy

Lots of hair is sexy too, if it's glossy and shiny. Legs
that are kept stubble-free and moisturised are lethal.
Good, well manicured nails work, as do long dark
eyelashes. Haven't got them? Buy them. Women in
beauty salons are throwing themselves into the road to
help you wear make-up. Fashion magazines appear
every month to help you dress.

*Someone who laughs a lot is sexy. I saw my girlfriend
in a pub, laughing out loud. She looked so happy and free.
I had to get to know her.'*

JAMIE, THIRTY

Do everything you can to look your best. Why? To
please men? *No.* To please yourself. Forget caring and
sharing to feel sexy you have to be selfish. The
grooming tips work because they make you feel good.
It's impossible to feel suicidal if you've just had a
manicure. Forget basket-weaving – I'd give manic
depressives an eyelash curler and a lipstick.

Flirting

After you've gotten your look, you'll need to work it. To be specific, you'll need to flirt. If looking good is the machine-gun of sexiness, flirting is the nuclear warhead. Men seem to know this already, and will spend hours charming a one-legged old lady for no other reason than it's fun. They, of course, think about sex an average of six times a minute. Which is a target you should aim for.

What is flirting? It's being open and friendly and warm. It's not giving a slow drop-wink and a leering smile that says, 'Meet you in the car park in ten.' Flirt with everyone, but especially with your partner. Like snogging, wearing sexy underwear and paying for dinner, flirting is the first thing to go when relationships move from New to Steady. But it shouldn't. Start flirting with them today. Send a text message saying 'You're gorgeous'.

Want a sure-fire flirting technique? Find a hapless male and talk to him about something general. But gaze deeply into his eyes while you do it. Really deeply. One eye, then the other. It'll slay him. But be warned: He might get an overwhelming urge to kiss you. Pick your target carefully.

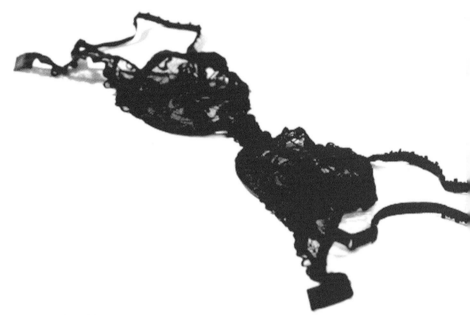

So... By now you should be acting like a sex goddess, dressing better, smiling more and flirting outrageously with everyone including the octogenarian in the post room. Despite your bumps, you should be feeling that your body is actually OK, and you might not quite need to fuse all the street lamps before you get naked. I'm proud of you. And you're ready to move on to the physical stuff.

LET'S GET PHYSICAL

To be orgasmic, you need to know how everything
works down there. So have a read, and get to grips
with the physical nitty gritty.

2

Vaginas – a user's guide

Knowing your vagina helps you to discover ways to stimulate it and how to masturbate. You do not have to be able to pick it out in an identity parade. Just feel your way. Masturbation is the first step to becoming orgasmic. Most women have their first climaxes alone, when they feel free to explore themselves, try different things and flail about wildly – without the distraction of an anxious boyfriend looking up over his aching shoulder every five minutes, saying, 'Anything?...'

The run up to orgasm...

1. *Arousal*

You know that achy, empty feeling you get during long snogging sessions? That's caused by the first stage of your sexual cycle – arousal. Blood flows down into your pelvis, plumping your lips and making your vagina darker in colour. And you'll start lubricating.

2. *Plateau*

You don't feel this stage so much, but it's all happening inside you. The top third of your vagina opens up, and

---

TRY THIS NOW!

Hold your labia wide open with one hand, rub your clitoris gently with the other. With the skin stretched tight like this, the feeling is intensified.

---

your womb shifts upwards slightly. This is your body putting the crisps and snacks out to meet the sperm.

3. *Climax*

Blood rushes to the chest making nipples harden and breasts get bigger. Hurrah! Clitoris becomes erect and painfully sensitive to touch. The labia swell. The muscles of the vagina contract and release spasmodically. Anus goes into spasm, heartbeat and breathing rate increase.

4. *Resolution*

The last stage of the cycle sees the body getting back to normal. Blood flows away from the pelvis, your breasts return to their normal size – sorry about that – and you feel happier and more relaxed. The increased blood pressure from the previous stages leaves a flush on your chest and face.

Masturbation

Hands up everyone who masturbates. (No. Not up there.) None of you? Hmmm. Well, the official figure is 64 per cent of women (and a huge 92 per cent of men). Quite a low figure when you consider how easy, pleasurable and relaxing masturbation is, how inexpensive, how low in calories. But it's true that some women do have mixed feelings about going Hans Solo.

Guilt is a common but groundless fear. There is absolutely nothing wrong with enjoying the pleasures of your own body. In fact, it's healthy.

'My orgasms vary, depending on whether I'm alone or with a partner. Alone, I tend to concentrate on stimulating my clitoris, so the orgasms are shorter and sharper. There's a long build up, while I'm flicking through my mental fantasies, trying to find the one that'll make me come. When I feel the orgasm is about to happen, I nearly stop breathing. I'm so tense, rubbing myself really hard, desperately trying to get over that cliff. Then, I do! A sudden, quick spasm I can feel all around my pubic area, then it's all over.'

KELLY, THIRTY-THREE

Masturbation health benefits

❀ Women who masturbate to orgasm regularly (once a week or more) have a greater number of orgasms during sex than women who rarely masturbate.

❀ Masturbation is recommended by psycho-sexual therapists to help women realize that fulfilment doesn't come only from men.

❀ An hour of masturbating to orgasm gives you a great cardiovascular workout.

❀ It releases endorphins, and reduces stress.

❀ It's truly Safe Sex.

❀ The more exercised your vaginal muscles, the less chances of complications during childbirth.

❀ It tones your upper arms.

How to do it

Lying down, standing up, on your side; fantasizing, not
fantasizing; reading or watching pornography; using pillows,
fingers, vibrators... These are a few of my favourite things.
There are no right or wrong ways to please yourself – it's
whatever turns you on. Really. Don't think in terms of 'dirty'
or 'weird'. If you want to push pebbles up your punani or
rub your bum with sandpaper, it's OK.

   To achieve orgasm, there are several main zones to
concentrate on – the clitoris, vagina, G-spot, A-spot and
Urethra. The following tricks and techniques are toe-curlingly
effective for most women.

SCIENTIFIC BIT

*When your oestrogen levels peak, at around day eighteen of your
menstrual cycle, you're at your most desirable. At that time of the
month your body produces extra pheromones (undetectable
hormones passed into the air via your sweat) that attract
surrounding men. You are 'on heat', and seriously sexy. Go forth
and pull, vixen.*

Clitoris
Up & down

Rest the heel of your hand on your mons pubis, where your pubic hair starts. Hold the top of your clitoris in between your index and middle finger, and rub up and down. Squeeze the outer lips together with your other hand.

How it works: Stimulates clitoris without pushing too hard on its ultra-sensitive tip. Also works the arms of the clitoris that extend down the labia.

Up & down, in & out

As above, but insert the thumb of the other hand just inside your vagina. Rub it around just inside your vaginal opening in smooth, circular movements.

How it works: Clitoral stimulation, and pleasures the cluster of nerves just inside the vagina.

The hump

Lie on your front in bed. Clench your thighs and knees together then rub your pelvis up and down along the mattress or pillow.

G-spot: beckon call

Lie on your back and curl your knees up onto your chest. Slide two fingers inside you, fingers curled up to the vaginal wall nearest your tummy. About 4 cm up is the G-spot, a patch of skin (about the size of a 50p) that feels spongy. This is erectile tissue: meaning it hardens and swells. Rub it in a 'come here' beckoning motion and a clockwise swirling motion, keeping the pressure gentle but consistent.

A-spot: higher, higher

As above, but run your fingers up the front wall until they reach your cervix. It feels like a firm lump (or the end of a nose). Midway between your cervix and your G-spot you'll find a smooth, extremely sensitive area (about the size of a 10p). A-ha! That's your A-spot. Slide a finger up and down it.

How it works: Reaches the A-spot, which is somewhat hard to get at.

Urethra: the waterfall

Press one finger onto the urethra (where urine exits the body) using firm, circular motions.

How it works: Many women find stimulation of their urethra can make them come. Not surprising, as it's slap-bang in the middle of the clitoris and the vagina. Most pleasurable when combined with clitoral stimulation.

If the Earth is not moving while your fingers are:

❀ *You're holding your breath*

This happens when you tense up, waiting to have an orgasm. But it can stop you coming. Concentrate on keeping your breathing slow and steady (that goes for when you're having sex too).

❀ *You're too dry*

Masturbation is a contact sport, so a lubricant is essential. Dip your finger inside yourself regularly while masturbating. Or use a water-based lubricant.

❀ *You're not relaxed enough*

You have to feel 'safe' to orgasm. So find somewhere private and comfortable where you won't be disturbed, and it'll be easier to let go. Take the phone off the hook and draw the curtains.

❀ *Or you're too relaxed*

Bored, madam? You might be a drama queen who needs extra excitement. So... masturbate in the loos at work. Practise stealthy handiwork on the bus or in

your car. Play with yourself in front of a window.
Spice it up.

❀ *Your period's due*

Hormone levels affect your sex drive and ability to
reach an orgasm. Oestrogen is the offender. On the
first day of your period oestrogen begins to build up
in your body. When it peaks (between day eleven
and day eighteen of your cycle), an egg is released
from one of your ovaries. You're now at your most
fertile and, cunningly, most lustful. Masturbation
would be good now. After day eighteen, oestrogen
levels fall until, about two days before your period is
due, you feel about as horny as a eunuch.

❀ *Your mind is wandering*

Use outside stimulus to focus your thoughts on sex.
Women's brains are aroused more by words than
pictures (men's are the opposite), so an erotic book
like *My Secret Garden* or *Men In Love*, both by
Nancy Friday should start a fire in your thong.

Alternative orgasms

Orgasms don't always require genital stimulation. It's possible to orgasm by breast massage, kissing, nipple-sucking, anal massage or foot-rubbing. Think outside your box. It's even possible to have a 'fantasy orgasm', achieved just by thinking, no touching required. Or, by stimulating two different parts of the body at once, you can intensify the sensation. For example, massage your clitoris and

'I lie on my side in bed. Then I reach one hand round behind me, slip my fingers inside my pussy and tickle my clitoris with the other hand. When I want to come I swirl my fingers around just inside my vagina, about an inch in. That seems to hit all the nerves and — bingo!'

KATIE, EIGHTEEN

your G-spot simultaneously, or your breasts and your A-spot. The idea is to work on more than one set of nerves, so the pleasurable sensations occur over a wider area.

Tool Box

Vibrators, Basic

When you buy your first vibrator, start small with a simple, handbag-sized example. Hold it directly against your clitoris for maximum sensation, or against your labia for a gentle touch. Perfect if you've never had an orgasm through masturbation.

Vibrators, Advanced

The supermodel of vibrators is the Eroscillator. Comes with four different heads to use on different erogenous zones; mains-powered (so it won't go flat on you at a crucial moment) and quiet. Heaven on a stick.

Rampant Rabbit

What Charlotte fell in love with on *Sex And The City*. It's a vibrating dildo with a clitoral stimulator built in. If you loved *Watership Down*, you'll love this.

G-Spot Vibrator

Hits the spot. No more searching for the perfectly-bent banana in the supermarket.

Love Eggs

Small, weighted balls that are inserted into your vagina. When you move, they click and clack about inside you and feel really rather lovely.

Lubricants

Choose water-based lubes – oil-based ones dissolve condoms and can irritate your genitals, causing thrush.

Clit Ticklers

Small and discreet, these battery-powered beauties are held directly against your clitoris, where their rubber nodules cause happy havoc.

Ribbed Condoms

Not just for intercourse, ribbed condoms can be slipped over anything that you might want to... accidentally fall onto while you weren't wearing pants. Honest, nurse. They also protect you from germs. But not splinters – so stay off that broomstick.

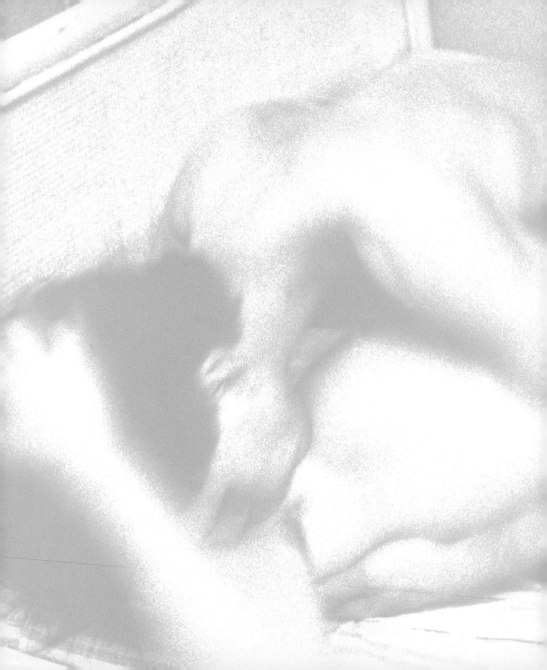

COMING TOGETHER

Truth is, having orgasms isn't all that difficult. (You should have made that blissful discovery in the last chapter.) But having orgasms during sex? Even the A-Team would balk at such an assignment. So read on…

3

Avoid sex-lag

A man can orgasm within three minutes of becoming excited; women need a minimum of thirteen minutes. So if you're going to stand a chance of orgasming before he does, you'll need foreplay. Snogging, massaging, teasing – anything that gets your motor running is essential. It's tempting to fast-forward to the moment of penetration – grabbing his penis and dragging it down to your pelvis before he's even parked the car – but that's a mistake. Remember: the less sighing and moaning you do before the shag, the more you'll do after. OK?

'I love being on top of my boyfriend. I tease him before we start. I straddle him and move my hips up over his mouth, let him kiss me, then trail my wet bits down over his chest, thighs and legs. When I do eventually shag him, he goes nuts.'

DIANE, THIRTY-THREE

Masturbate before the date

As Katie reveals: 'My boyfriend once told me that he often masturbates before he sees me so he can last longer in bed. I do too, but for the opposite reason.

Before he arrives I play with myself until just before I climax, then stop. It gets me so aroused that I come really quickly when we fuck.'

Masturbate during the date

If you aren't in the habit of masturbating while you shag, you're missing a trick. Direct clitoral stimulation is the easiest way to come. In fact, the sight of a woman taking her orgasm into her own hand is the sexiest sight they can imagine. The more evolved males will do it for you. But if not, pinch your clitoris between first and middle fingers, press down and make circular motions.

SCIENTIFIC BIT

When you orgasm, your body releases a hormone called oxytin, which makes you feel happy and relaxed. It also bonds you to your partner. Women release about five times more of it than men do, which is why we can become sexually addicted to a man. Once bonded, it takes a full two years of cold-turkey – no sexual contact with him at all – for your body to recover.

Top sex positions:
guaranteed show-stoppers

10/10 *Women on top:* facing forwards

Straight in at Number One is the golden oldie of sex positions. You or your lover can play with your clitoris and your madly bouncing breasts. For G-spot action, sit down and lean backwards: his penis will rub against the front wall of your vagina. For A-spot action, do the same, and 'rock' backwards and forwards, keeping his penis in as deep as it'll go. (Not so stimulating for men, so intersperse with some up-down thrusts or he could lose his hard-on.)

Variations: squat over him like a jockey, feet flat on the bed and bounce up and down. Great for hitting the nerves around your vaginal opening; bad for getting him so aroused he comes in a nanosecond.

Stimulates: clitoris, G-spot, A-spot, breasts.

9/10 *Women on top:* facing his feet

Trickier than position one, but worth it. His penis is bent forwards so that it rubs against your G-spot and A-spot. You can reach down to your clitoris (and play with his testicles, if he's been good) and he can rub your anus.

Variations: pull his toes when he's coming. It extends his orgasm.

Stimulates: clitoris, G-spot, A-spot, anus.

'I first saw this in a dirty film, and couldn't wait to try it. It's not easy — you have to be careful not to bend too far forward or it'll hurt him or "pop" his penis out. But the feelings it gives me are awesome.'

ANDREA, TWENTY-FOUR

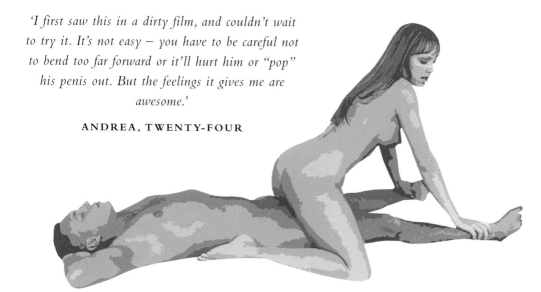

9/10 *Missionary no. 1:* he kneels up, you lie face-up on bed, knees bent up

When I die I want to be buried like this. It hits everything. As he has his hands full holding your legs, you should reach down and rub your clitoris, or hold your lips closed around his penis. Nurse!

Variations: if he pulls up your hips (by raising your legs with his arms), he'll increase his pressure on your G-spot.

Stimulates: clitoris, G-spot.

'This is by far my husband's and my fave position. I love the feeling of "fullness" it gives me. We have to be careful not just to do this every time.'

JULIET,
TWENTY-SEVEN

8/10 *Missionary no. 2: C.A.T.*

The C.A.T. position stands for Coital Alignment
Technique – but I prefer to think it got its name
because eight out of ten pussies prefer it. It's like
missionary, except your man moves up until his
shoulders are past yours. He then braces his feet on
something – the bed, or a friendly passer-by. This way,
the base of his penis remains slightly out of you and
presses against your clitoris. Happy birthday! With
shallower thrusts – more of a rocking motion – he'll
rub your clitoris with every move. Grrrr.

Variations: he can circle his hips instead of thrusting,
keeping that constant pressure on your pubic bone.

Stimulates: clitoris.

*'You have to teach the man how to do this, as it's not his
usual "mad pushing" action. But once you do, it's heaven.
The orgasms I achieve in this position are really deep –
they grow slowly and steadily until I just erupt down there.'*

SINITA, TWENTY-ONE

'My man's penis is short and very thick, so this is excellent for us. It gives me a "filled-up" sensation!'

**JACKIE,
TWENTY-SEVEN**

5-7/10 *Missionary no. 3:* legs bent up, feet over man's shoulders

The reason the rating varies on this one is because some women love deep vaginal penetration like this, and some don't. The only thing to do is try it! With your legs up over his shoulders, you won't find it easy to stimulate your clitoris. So concentrate on his deeper thrustings. Having the cervix rubbed like this can induce intense vaginal orgasms.

Variations: he can hold your feet and push your legs right back over your head. Very deep thrusts.

Stimulates: vaginal nerves.

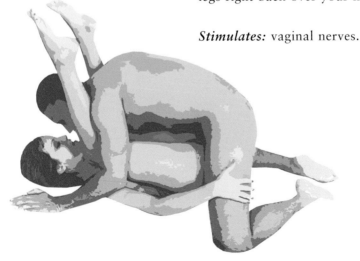

7/10 *Spooning:* face-to-face

Lie on your sides facing each other. When he inserts
his penis you can squeeze your thighs together to get a
'tighter' feeling. His body rubs against your clitoris in
a very pleasing manner, and he lasts a long time.

Variations: he can lie behind you and enter that way,
while you play with your clitoris.

Stimulates: clitoris.

'We discovered spooning from behind when I was pregnant.
Now I like it when we're face to face. It's intimate, and it rubs
on my clitoris.'

SALLY, THIRTY-NINE

7/10 *Standing up:* him standing, her sitting on table, her legs round his waist

When you buy a bed, try to get one that's very high. Then you can have loads of fun! When you're sitting, facing your man, legs around his waist, his penis is pushed right up against the nerves near your cervix. Result: deep vaginal orgasms.

Variations: bend your legs up against his chest. Deep, man, deep.

Stimulates: vaginal nerves.

'Our best shags are in the kitchen, when my boyfriend sits me up on the work-top and enters me. There's something about this angle that makes me feel really narrow, and his cock feels massive. He rests his thumb against my clitoris too, which speeds up my orgasm.'

TRICIA, TWENTY-NINE

7/10 *Good dog*

Rear-entry positions are good for G-spot orgasms, as
the man's penis is pushed up against that front wall.
Men love it too (which is nice) and it's especially good
for girls with larger vaginas (like if they've had a baby).
You can vary the angle by putting pillows under your
stomach, or standing up and bending over.

Variations: stand up and put your hands
on the floor, or hold onto a low
stool. This arches your back and
heightens the G-spot
stimulation.

Stimulates: G-spot, A-spot.

*'My fave, fave position.
It's dirty and passionate.
This is a "fuck", not
"lovemaking".'*

**SUZANNAH,
THIRTY-ONE**

Thou must not fake

What? Not even when he's been toiling away
in there for hours, you're red-raw, desperate for
sleep but know he won't come until you do?
Nope. Not even then. I'm saying this after years
of being an Oscar-worthy actress. The only thing
to do when you're feeling about as orgasmic as,
as – an ashtray, is to tell him. Something sweet
like, 'You're the sexiest man and I love what
you're doing. But it's just not going to happen
for me tonight.' Then help him through the
finishing post, pick up your knitting and relax.
That way, he doesn't feel too bad, but he also
doesn't try exactly the same technique next time.

Of course, one reason why we do feel like
faking is when the man is doing something
wrong. Or not wrong, exactly, but just not quite
right. This is common with new partners, who
sometimes assume that what drove their ex wild
in bed will drive you mad too. The last thing
you want to do in that situation is pretend.

Instead, learn how to say what you like while
still making him feel manly. There are two ways.
The first is to lead with praise: be very loudly

appreciative when he does something you like, but stay silent when he does something you don't. Men love pleasing you, and he'll soon concentrate on the techniques that got you screaming last time, and drop the ones that didn't.

The second is to ask him if he'd like you to show him what turns you on. Pick your moment – before sex is ideal, afterwards isn't. Wait until he says yes – he will – and then show him. Place his hands where you want them. Kiss him as you want to be kissed. And touch yourself a lot. It'll turn him on and the lesson will soon turn into a shag-fest. (Trust me, I've lost whole weekends like this).

SCIENTIFIC BIT

When asked to describe their ideal sex partner, men listed 'insatiable', 'highly sexed' and 'demanding' as their favourite qualities. All the more reason for you to get pro-active in bed. Only weeny, wimpy guys are scared by take-charge temptresses.

Intercourse orgasms

'It's much easier for me to come when I'm on top of the man. Grinding my hips around in circular motions makes his penis touch all the important areas.'

MARY, THIRTY

'I can't come from sex alone. I either have to play with myself at the same time, or use visual stimulus like having a porn film playing in the room. I think it freaks the men out slightly. But why? I know loads of women who can't get there from shagging.'

BECKY, THIRTY-ONE

'I had a boyfriend who used to fake orgasms. He'd wear condoms, and then whisk them away before I could notice they were empty. I eventually confronted him and he said he sometimes felt pressure to perform, and that I wasn't turning him on. Since then, I've never faked. It's pointless. I'd rather finish the relationship if the sex wasn't up to scratch.'

JULES, THIRTY

Use props

A great way to get more out of your shags is to use props.
We'll go into adventurous sex later, but in the meantime,
stock your bedroom with these. Then play around with
them. You'll be surprised how horny you can feel just by
putting a pillow under your bum and watching yourself in
a mirror.

❀ Mirrors

❀ Waist-high bed – so he can enter you standing up

❀ Chair – sit on top of him

❀ Lighting – candles can turn cellulite into
    celluloid-standard

❀ Pillows (under bum)

❀ Stuff to hang onto – bed-heads are great for helping
    you maintain tricky positions

❀ Water – try the bath for a wet and wild experience

Toys

Penile shafts

These look like condoms with the ends swan off. Thick, usually ribbed or studded, they slip over your lover's penis to increase its girth. They're blissful to use, but can do more damage to your lover's ego than getting 'Pin-Prick' printed on his T-shirt.

'The length of our shags tended to dwindle after an extremely short time until my partner discovered the cock ring. He now manages to keep an erection for up to three or four times as long.'

MARIE, TWENTY-NINE

Cock ring

Metal rings that slip over the penis and testicles. They hold the blood in, lengthening his erection time. Worth a try if your man's erections tend to wither away without warning.

'We got really aroused whilst preparing dinner one evening and decided to do it there and then on the counter top so we had to improvise and use olive oil as a lubricant.'

DAISY, THIRTY-THREE

Condoms

Condom manufacturers are now making endless different types to encourage us to use them. I say, do! You can get them studded, knobbled, ribbed... avoid flavoured though, a friend once tried them and was horrified the next day to find her pants full of a yellow, banana-scented melted mess.

Love beads

String of plastic beads that are pushed up the man's bum during a shag, then pulled out as he comes. Stimulate the prostate gland, which is his G-spot. Can hurt. Do not attempt to use when you're pre-menstrual and punchy.

Lubricants

You know the lubricant I urged you to masturbate with? Well, use it on him too. KY Jelly can have the effect of numbing him slightly, so he goes on longer.

HOW TO RECEIVE PLEASURE

This is all about teaching him how to please us girls. So make sure you leave this book open at chapter four on your coffee table! Yes guys, that's you we're talking about, get reading.

4

Calling all men

❀ Where is the most sensitive part of our body (and no, it's not the clitoris)?

❀ How can you get more sex, without begging, cheating or paying?

❀ What is the one sure-fire way of turning a girl on?

If you've ever wanted to know the answers to questions like these, this is the chapter for you. If you're reading it, it's probably because your girlfriend has left the book lying open at this page somewhere she knows you'll spot it – like in the fridge, for example, her knicker drawer, or in her dirty-underwear basket.

SCIENTIFIC BIT

To get stronger erections for longer – and still be getting jiggy aged ninety – do 'press ups'. When erect, lift your penis up towards your stomach and back down, using your pelvic muscles. To make it harder, push against it with your hand.

'We like hand-jobs too. Slip your hand into our pants when we're watching TV, and gently rub our clitoris with a wet thumb. Bliss.'

MARTHA, TWENTY-THREE

She's not telling you you're bad in bed. In fact, she's telling you that you're good, because only truly sexy men are open to discovering new techniques. This is a compliment, darling. And by the time you've read this, you'll receive millions more.

What turns women on

'A man has to have sex to feel good; a woman has to feel good to have sex.'

Get that quote lodged in your brain and you'll die a happy, very tired old man, probably at the end of a three-week shagathon.

Women's sex-drive starts in their brain, in that little part which controls how attractive and desirable they feel. In truth, women will find you sexy if you obviously find them sexy. They will not find you sexy if they feel you only want them because they're the only naked woman in the bedroom.

In fact, without feeling sexy, a woman cannot orgasm. When she should be lying there concentrating on how expertly you're manhandling her nethers, she is in fact analyzing your relationship and wondering if you secretly fancy her flatmate. So, if your partners consistently fail to achieve the big O, take a look at your relationship skills. Could you be more protective, cherishing, attentive and warm? If so, *be* those things. This is what all those old-time lotharios knew. Casanova didn't spend his life working on how to make his penis bigger. Instead, he wrote love letters; he complimented women; he called them beautiful; he remembered their birthdays. In response, they felt sexy and wanted, they associated him with feeling good about themselves, they fell into bed, and they orgasmed.

Make it plain you find your lover sexy. Call her at work and tell her she's gorgeous. Kiss her a lot, all the time, everywhere. (Astonishing how quickly couples stop snogging – madness when you consider it is the best way to get an erection, and start the

'Don't touch us how you like to be touched. We're more sensitive. We love butterfly-soft, light strokes, not deep rubs. Basically, do it so gently that you reckon we won't feel it. That should be spot-on.'

KATHY, THIRTY-TWO

'When I beg him to enter me, I often don't mean it. It's better if the man puts off penetration until you're both desperate for it. I know it makes him more likely to come quickly, but it makes me more likely to as well. Teasing is the ultimate turn on.'

SANDY, TWENTY-THREE

'Those women in dirty films who fake these huge screaming orgasms are doing us all a disservice! I want one of the porn-star women to sit up and say to the man "You'll have to do better than that, buddy".'

MARIA, FORTY

lady lubricating.) Wolf-whistle when she runs naked across the bedroom. Start every date by saying, 'Hey, have you lost weight?' (a cheap shot that, but infallible).

Of course, you shouldn't be a woman's confidence-boost. She has to get that from herself. But it will never hurt if you openly show her how beautiful and sexy you find her. (Well, it might, actually. But only in your broken back and exhausted elbows.) And, if you need another reason, it will make her orgasm so loudly your neighbours will look at you with new respect in the morning.

SCIENTIFIC BIT

Does size matter? Yes, but not in the way you think. The perfect penis for stimulating a woman is not long and thick. It's short and stubby. The nerve endings are thickest around the inside of the vaginal opening. Very long penises can jab against the cervix and hurt. If your penis is narrow, doggy-style is your best position. Aim upwards, and you'll rub against her G-spot.

TRY THIS NOW!

Lick your lover's vagina from behind. Although it's harder for you to reach her clitoris, it feels dirty and erotic. 'Animal' was the way most women described it.

How to undress her

Slowly is usually best. With sharp intakes of breath and lustful moans every time a pointy bit springs out. If you sense she hates her body, compliment her more. With enough confidence, a woman would lap dance for you on an open-top bus. If it's a quickie, concentrate on removing your clothes while she tears off hers. Watch her as she does, and drool a bit. Why? Again, to help her become orgasmic. Doing things slowly and seductively will help a woman relax – women have to be relaxed to be able to come. We're not like you: men seem to be born with sexual confidence. You always have to stop yourselves coming; we have to learn how to *start*. You can help us.

Foreplay

We need lots. In fact, we need about twice as much as you think we do, plus a few hours. Foreplay, to girls, is everything. It gets us into gear, it starts us lubricating, it increases our sensitivity to touch, and it even changes the shape of our vaginas so we're better designed to greet your penis. Without foreplay, we physically can't orgasm. Unlike boys, we don't spend every 6 seconds thinking about sex. (That's your foreplay, and you do it every day. No wonder you can come easily.) So, we need you to 'sex us up', mentally.

'Lubrication is a must. Sex hurts when I'm not wet enough. My ex used to pretend to chew gum to get his saliva glands working. It was perfect!'

JULIA, TWENTY-NINE

Perfect kissing
Mouth

Again, this is about looking carried away. So touch her face a lot, stroke the back of her neck and hold her chin. That's so hot. We like build-up, so lick her bottom lip gently. Slowly suck her tongue into your

mouth, or suck her bottom lip. Plant butterfly-kisses on her eyelids (we adore that, but men never do it). And wait until she has made the first tongue-move before you do. She'll get more excited.

Ears

Most women don't like having tongues pushed into their ears. I know you do, but we (usually) don't. It's a medical fact that men's ears are more erogenous (just like they're hairier). Instead, lick around the ear, put your mouth right over it, then gently suck air in. It can turn her brain inside out.

Neck

A killer spot for almost all women. Kiss her on the sides of her neck, from underneath her earlobes down to the tops of her shoulders. Most girls find that immediately sets their crotches alight! Lift up her hair and kiss the back of her neck. Trail your tongue down her spine to the curve just above her buttocks – another killer area. The skin on our neck and back is thinner and sensitive to all kinds of touches. Experiment.

Breast action

Do not squeeze them like oranges, push them together, or pinch the nipples like bubblewrap. Start gently (most women like lighter touches than men; our skin is thinner and more vulnerable) and leave the nipples till last. Hold your hands out flat and run your palms up and over the breasts. Stroke the underneath of them. Tease the nipples by circling round them with your light fingertips, until they're standing out like fat cigar butts.

Then lick upwards over the nipples, swirl lightly around the aureoles, and finally sip on the nipples. These are just suggestions – ask her what she likes. Some girls (me! me! me!) love having their nipples bitten; others hate it.

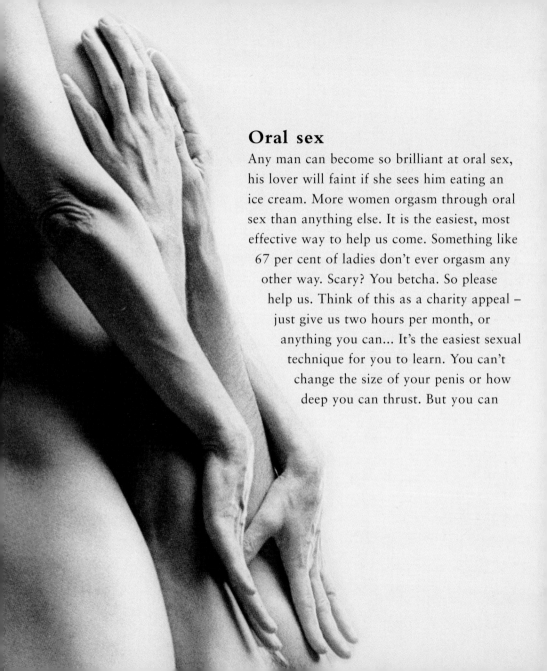

Oral sex

Any man can become so brilliant at oral sex,
his lover will faint if she sees him eating an
ice cream. More women orgasm through oral
sex than anything else. It is the easiest, most
effective way to help us come. Something like
67 per cent of ladies don't ever orgasm any
other way. Scary? You betcha. So please
help us. Think of this as a charity appeal –
just give us two hours per month, or
anything you can... It's the easiest sexual
technique for you to learn. You can't
change the size of your penis or how
deep you can thrust. But you can

change the way you lick, or the skill with which you pinpoint a clitoris. And it's those things which can help your partner let go and start to experience the biggest orgasms she's ever had.

Positions

A good all-rounder is her lying back, you kneeling between her legs. Use pillows – some under her bottom, some under your chest. It's makes the job much easier. If you can rest your head on her thigh occasionally it'll relieve your neck and make saliva 'pool' in your mouth, giving you the wetness we love. If you want her to sit on your face, have her lean her arms on the bed-head. She can move her hips better, and get you right where she wants you!

TRY THIS NOW!

Have him masturbate you with a ice-pop. It feels great and will drive him mad when he gets to shag your icy cold bits.

Hairs

Check you're not too stubbly. (Rub your chin on your wrist. If it hurts, get a shave.) And remove any stray hairs from her bush by stroking it first.

Make some noise!

Women hate silent lovers. We hate them. But they're everywhere! I can't tell you the times I've held a mirror over a lover's face just to see if he were alive. I know why you're the strong, silent type: you're concentrating on the action; you feel silly; and moaning turns you on and you're afraid you'll come. True? Well, here's a tip: we'd rather you came too quickly because you were excited, rather than grimly sawing away for hours.

SCIENTIFIC BIT

Some women can orgasm just by having their breasts massaged. And so can some men, although not many. (Less than 1 per cent of the population, on estimate.)

Techniques

❀ Her clitoris is very like the head of your penis (it even has a hood, like your foreskin) and responds to the same kind of stimulation. So don't flick! Sharp, stabby tongue-flicks are irritating and deadening – like they are to you. Instead, smother her clitoris in your wet, loose mouth and suck on it gently.

❀ Swirl a flat, wet tongue all around her vagina.

❀ Lick up and down her lips, then swirl your tongue just inside her vagina.

❀ Hold her clitoris gently in your mouth and 'hum' on her. Goooood vibrations.

❀ Use your fingers. Place one hand above her pubic bone, flat on her skin, and press it upwards. It'll open her up and lift her clitoris out from under its hood.

❀ Some girls love it when you hold their clitoris in your mouth and shake your head from side to side very fast. (This leaves me cold, however. I'm just saying.)

❀ Place one finger either side of her clitoris and make circular motions.

❀ Dip your thumb into her vagina, just inside.

❀ Reach two fingers into her about five centimetres up, and make 'come here' beckoning motions against the front (tummy-side) wall. It should hit her G-spot – you'll know when, as it'll feel smoother than the rest of her vaginal walls, and she'll go mad!

❀ Suck gently on her clitoris while you slide two fingers in and out of her.

❀ Bend your index and middle fingers in half, then 'shag' her with them.

❀ Have her masturbate her clitoris while you lick around it. Very hot!

❀ Lick her anus.

Read her responses

❀ When she starts moaning, keep doing what you're doing. Don't swap to a different technique. We need sustained stimulation.

❀ When she raises her legs and pulls your head closer into her, she wants more pressure.

❀ When she tenses up and stops breathing, she is either about to come or has heard her husband walking up the stairs.

TRY THIS NOW!

If her breasts are too small to give you a breast-masturbation have her wear a wonderbra. Smother her boobs in lubricant, and slip your penis in between her new, improved cleavage.

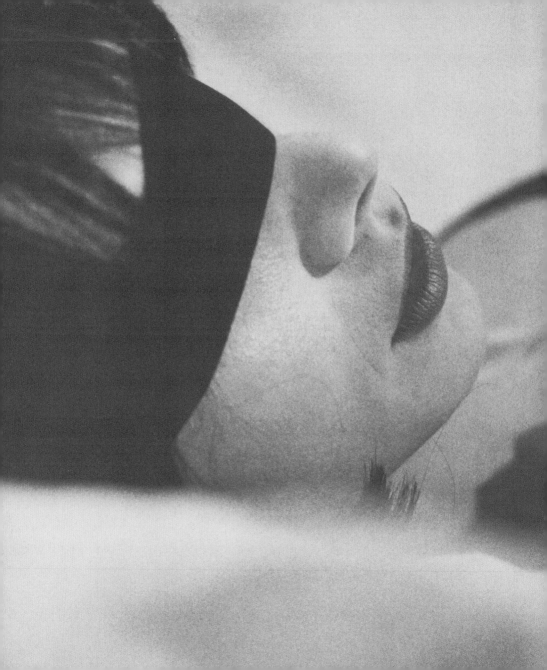

USING
FANTASY
TO ORGASM

Fantasies are to orgasms what breasts are
to page-three girls: Essential.

5

The secret truth about fantasies

Whether it's the impure thoughts you have on the way to work, or the Brad Pitt makeover you give to your boyfriend during sex, fantasies can help you reach the big O no end.

Need proof? Then think about this: 78 per cent of women admitted they needed sexual fantasy to help them orgasm during sex; and 99 per cent needed it when masturbating.

Why fantasize?

Fantasies free your mind, and help it focus on sex. As we've already discussed, that's *essential* for women as our brains are so often jam-packed with other stuff – body-image, insecurity, shopping lists – that we just can't feel sexy. Fantasies are also your own private world, where you get free rein to think about anything arousing without having to justify, explain, or watch a horrified lover back out of the bedroom. That's vital to orgasm, because only you know your on/off switch. Whether it's two nuns in a bikini, or a bulldog in rollerblades, dirty thoughts can tip the balance and help you orgasm.

How do I fantasize?

If you think you've never fantasized, you're probably mistaken. It doesn't have to be a full-blown Hollywood production, with dance numbers and a chorus line. It could be a fleeting image of your lover going down on you. Fantasies are essentially just rude thoughts. In fact, men's fantasies tend to be much better thought-out than women's. The women's are brief and basic ('I often imagine I am being raped by my husband as he is making love to me'). But the men's... Phew! Even Stephen Spielberg couldn't compare for scripts, costume changes and dialogue. But you needn't compete: just give yourself full license to go as detailed and as dirty as you need.

Pick a time when you won't be disturbed, and somewhere you can be naked. (Eventually you can fantasize anywhere, I still have fond fondling memories of the office toilets. I think I left footprints on the back of the cubicle door.) Lie still, and let your hands explore your body while your mind explores your fantasies. Think of anything, or lots of things. Images of attractive men touching you... attractive women touching you... attractive gerbils running over your breasts... *Anything* goes. The secret is to think of loads of different images until you discover one that makes you aroused. Got one? Then expand on it. If it's a sexy stranger shagging you in the rain, backtrack a bit. Imagine him meeting you, smiling at you... Picture what you're wearing, and how he removes it. Visualize you seducing him, or straddling his face... While you do, touch yourself more. Try the masturbation techniques in Chapter two.

You might run out of steam before you've orgasmed. If so, then just replay the fantasy. Or add more characters. The trick is to let your thoughts reach a crescendo as your orgasm does. Think of it like rewinding a porn film over and over until you orgasm at your favourite scene. (What? You've never watched one? Then keep reading, sweetie! We've got treats in store for you.)

TRY THIS NOW!

Write your own erotic fiction: type out a filthy, made-up story starring your man and yourself. (Disguised, if you're scared someone will read it.) Leave it under his pillow one night. He'll love it. Just be careful not to get literal – describe his penis as 'massive' and 'engorged', not 'of baby snail proportions'.

'When I told Dean my fantasy of being shagged by Dracula in a gothic castle, I thought he'd laugh at me. Instead, it really turned him on. He kept asking for more details – was Dracula wearing a cape? Did he bite my neck? It turned us on enough to have great sex that night. But even more, Dean actually acted it out. He took me away for the weekend to a gorgeous old rambling castle in Leeds, then surprised me by coming out of the bathroom in vampire get-up. I was flattered – and aroused. We shagged all night, and I had the biggest orgasms ever. It was so sexy seeing it come true.'

HELEN, TWENTY-SEVEN

'I've always fancied a threesome, so when my fiancé told me he'd once had one, I was happily surprised. I thought, here's the bloke who'll finally have one with me without getting jealous! But, when it came to it, he started suggesting friends of mine who he'd want one with. I freaked out totally. I think they're too dangerous. I'd only have one with two strangers.'

CAROLINE, TWENTY-NINE

Helping hands

Sometimes, your own mind just can't come up with the thoughts that will help you get there. Or it can, but you still need more stimulation. If this is the case (and you'll know if it is, after three hours of masturbating has just left you with aching arms, a full answer machine of unreturned messages but still no orgasm), you'll need a helping hand. But not your lover's. (Not yet.) Instead, turn to erotic literature. The statistics on women reaching orgasm through reading erotic words are astounding – 68 per cent of women who subscribed to an American erotic fiction review said it helped them 'understand their sexual needs and improve their sex life'. Truth is, ladies are aroused by words. (Men prefer pictures.)

This has always been the case. Did you think your Mum read *Lady Chatterley's Lover* for plot? No way. But luckily, we have access to more erotic fiction than any other generation. Whole publishing companies are thriving on our love of erotic stories. They have something for every taste. So, if after exploring your brain and realizing that spanking arouses you, peruse your newsagent for a book on that topic. Or domination. Or lesbianism.

Whatever you like, you will find that an author has fleshed it out (so to speak) into a book. Once you've mastered fantasizing Hans Solo, you can incorporate them into sex.

Sharing your secret fantasies

'When I realized that I felt so safe and comfortable with John that I could tell him my most secret sexual fantasies, I knew he was Mr Right,' says Sally, thirty-four. 'I'd never have dreamt of telling my previous boyfriends anything so intimate. But with John, it was so easy.'

Great sex will only come with open, honest communication. How easily you can share your sex secrets will tell you a lot about your relationship. I say go for it, if you feel comfortable – it'll reveal your Secret Sex Language.

SCIENTIFIC BIT

Don't hold your breath, but the laws against showing erect penises are getting, er, softer. Expect to be able to see one in top-shelf magazines by 2003. I can't wait.

Secret Sex Language

Listen to the words you use when you're telling your
fantasy. Get specific. Do you say 'cock' or 'dick'?
'fuck' or 'shag'? These are the words that turn you on.
Remember them, and start thinking of them during
sex, or ask your lover to say them to you. Dirty words
help women orgasm. It's another way of pushing your
brain over the edge, and focusing your thoughts on sex.

Making fantasies come true

Once you've confessed your innermost fantasies, the
question will be hanging in the air above the bed:
Should you act them out? The answer's yes, if you are
sure the relationship will stay the same, or become
stronger, afterwards; you both want to, and aren't
doing it to please the other, or out of fear they'll leave
you if you don't. It's easy to get carried away wanting
your boyfriend to think you're the wildest, most
uninhibited lover they've ever met, but be careful. If
you let him tie you up in skipping-ropes and beat you
with an egg-whisk because you think he'll like it, then
you either start crying with shame or laughing at how
weird he is, you'll look spineless, not sassy. Believe me.
Been there, done that, still got the weals on my bum.

Pornography

Here's an interesting fact: human beings are the only species to use sexual fantasies to orgasm. All other creatures need visual stimulus while they masturbate – which means yes, the chimpanzee you saw masterbating in the zoo *was* looking at your breasts.

But, of course, humans do use outside stimulation too. Like... pornography. Now, I'm a great fan. If you're not, I can understand. It's never nice to know that your boyfriend gets aroused looking at gynaecological shots of other women. But, babycakes, he does. They all do. He gets tingles seeing a bra-less woman jogging; he might get a semi watching your Mum eat a banana – get over it! Instead of fuming and carting his dirty-magazine stash down to the tip, why not try it yourself?

TRY THIS NOW!

Put a blue-movie on TV and shag while it's playing. You'll find yourself taking on the actresses' sexy attitudes.

Magazines

These are my favourites, because of the Readers Letters
– sexual fantasies written down in explicit detail. Often
you'll be surprised how excited these can get you.
Again, don't feel weird. Enjoying reading about how a
seventeen-year-old schoolgirl was deflowered by a dinner
lady don't mean a thing (I hope...) And neither does
drooling over the pretty breasts.

Aural

If you've never recorded the sounds of your lovemaking
on a cassette, then replayed it back, I'm ashamed of
you. Do it *now*. Either play it back when you're
shagging (makes your bedroom sound like an orgy), or
before, to get you going. Very arousing, and might just
be the thing to help you climax.

Films

All the decent ones are banned, which means you'll
have to ask a man to lend you one of his. They seem to
have an underground network of them. Again, horny as
hell, but might make you paranoid about your body.
Those women are usually built like Cindy dolls – all
legs, tits and arms that come out on rubber bands

(from what I can see). The best ones are foreign (where they're legal), so you'll miss out on following the plot unless you're bi-cunnilingual.

The Ultimate...

For the ultimate pornographic experience, make your own blue-movie. But don't commit it to tape, rig the camera up to the TV, but do *not*, repeat, *not* put a tape in it. Just play it through the screen, like a TV studio monitor.

Wear your sexiest lingerie and light the room with candles. Have the screen in plain view of the bed. Do everything you can think of. Watching it on the screen as it happens is – well, see for yourself. You can get sooo carried away. I would say, 'Break a leg!' but really, I'm afraid you will.

Funnier fantasy stories:

*'I was always secretly ashamed by my fantasies. I'd been
making them up since I was about twelve and some had got
pretty involved. But my best friend Caroline, one night, over
drinks, admitted that she had some wild ones too. We
eventually persuaded each other to tell one. She was pretty
horrified by mine — it was a rape scenario, where I was a
red-haired virgin nun, aged sixteen (I said it was involved!)
— but I was disgusted by hers! She had this whole fantasy
built up about shagging in front of her younger brother, and
showing him how to have sex. I was scared at the time. But
still… later that night, at my house, I lay in bed and started
thinking about Caroline's fantasy. And well… it turned me
on so much that I masturbated, and reached a huge orgasm.
I almost phoned her up to thank her — but I guess some
things friends shouldn't share.'*

KATIE, TWENTY-EIGHT

'Fantasizing is the easiest way for me to orgasm. It doesn't have to be a specific thought, it can just be isolated body parts, or images of penises. Whatever it is, it is always enough to push me over the edge if my orgasm is taking too much time. But I do get carried away. Once I screamed out "Dicks! Yes! Dicks!" while my lover shagged me, which was kind of hard to explain.'

SUSAN, THIRTY-THREE

'My ex once wrote me a long love letter which contained a pretty detailed description of a shag. I was going off him at the time, so I was surprised how sexy I found it. It made me realise how sexy he thought I was — it had some lovely descriptions of my body — and I used it to masturbate with. I orgasmed three times to that letter. But I still dumped him a week later, though I never gave the letter back! I'd frame it, if I lived on my own...'

CANDIDA, THIRTY-ONE

ADVANCED

If you're not, by now, lying back in bed, exhausted,
and satisfied, you're just not trying. That's OK
though, because this is the chapter that will cause
your bed sheets to burst into flames. You are about to
learn the sort of exotic love-making techniques that
will give you orgasms so strong, you won't believe it.

6

This is where we go advanced, exotic – all mysterious and glam with your sex life. Building on the tricks you've already got under your belt from the previous chapters, this section is all about achieving unusual and unexpected orgasms.

We are going to take a look at Tantric orgasms, multiple orgasms and simultaneous orgasms... Yes girls, they can get bigger, better, stronger, wetter.

Simultaneous orgasms

Have you ever had a simultaneous orgasm with a partner? If you haven't, brace yourself. You're about to. If you have, you'll know exactly why it's being

TRY THIS NOW!

Girls, you can use toys to improve your PC muscles too! Try inserting a banana inside you, then gripping it as hard as you can. Stand up and walk around, using only those muscles to keep it in place. Then push hard until you can shoot it across the room.

covered in such detail here: Simultaneous orgasms
are *awesome*.

Even for a jaded old cynic like me, the feeling when
you come at exactly the same time as your lover is...
Well, lets call it whore-inspiring. Few things connect
you as beautifully, or leave you feeling as satisfied. It's
like a soul-mate connection if, ahem, you believe in that
kind of thing.

What makes it so inspiring is *exactly* what makes it
elusive: it is unpredictable, unplanned. Or, at least, it
was until now. Here you're about to learn just how to
achieve it, as often as you want to.

The trick to timing your orgasm to coincide with his,
is to know when you're going to come. Sounds simple?
Pah! How many times have you lingered on the brink of
an orgasm for hours, before it finally faded away into
nothing? Your body is a complicated machine. You have
to learn to read the manual to understand how it
works. But it can be done with a little preparation,
information and experimentation. Which you'll enjoy.
When you become able to tell exactly how aroused you
are (and how aroused your lover is too), you can almost
schedule your orgasms like flights.

Learn your arousal Levels

This is the first step. And it's fabulous. So, head off with your lover into the bedroom. The first stage is *you*. Have your man stimulate you for hours. Using the techniques in Chapter two would be good – you want steady clitoral stimulation, lots of touching and stroking. And lots of snogging – *nothing* is as good for raising your arousal.

While he is playing with you, concentrate on how aroused you feel and with practice, you'll learn the art of telling your levels.

When you've learned to spot the different Levels of arousal, then you must learn to control them. How? Easy. Just focus only on the sensations. First, read the list overleaf. Then identify the Level you're in and try to stay there. If your arousal moves down a gear and you're starting to get bored, think deliberately sexy thoughts, play with your breasts and stay with that until your arousal returns up. Or if you're getting more aroused and moving UP a Level, empty your mind and think un-sexy thoughts until it calms down. Soon, you'll know exactly how to control your arousal and then it is time to move onto him.

Top ten arousal levels

- ❀ **Level One** gently aroused

- ❀ **Level Two** more aroused, lubricated

- ❀ **Level Three** aroused, heavier breathing

- ❀ **Level Four** very aroused, clawing bed sheets

- ❀ **Level Five** head moving on pillow, slight groans

- ❀ **Level Six** louder groans

- ❀ **Level Seven** point of no return: tingling, beginnings of feeling orgasmic

- ❀ **Level Eight** very near orgasm, centred heat around pubic area

- ❀ **Level Nine** almost there

- ❀ **Level Ten** ORGASM

How to control Levels

When you're finally able to Name and Control your Levels from the list on the previous page, knowing when you're going to come should be easy. So the next trick is, getting your man to the same stage of experience.

Learn his arousal Levels

Play with your man as detailed previously, while he gets to discover how to name and control his Levels.
It might take a while. Bring sandwiches.

Learn each other's Levels

Once you're both masters of your arousal Levels, you have my permission to start practising for a

TRY THIS NOW!

To practise getting to know each other's arousal Level, play this game. One of you stimulates your partner in ways you know they especially like. Then try to guess which arousal Level they're in. The more you can recognize the other's desire, the better you'll be at coming together.

simultaneous orgasm. It's going to mean shagging. Maybe lots of shagging. Happy with that? Good. Then start shagging, but don't forget to tell each other which Level you're in. For example, you whimper, 'I'm at Level Nine! Keep going!' While he yawns, 'Naaah. Just Level Two for me, babe. Got any porn?'

This will teach you what each other's Levels actually look like. You'll soon learn, for example, that his Level Eight is when he breathes rapidly, and thrusts particularly deeper. His Level Nine might be when he begins whimpering, and Level Ten – well, that one speaks for itself. He, in turn, will learn that your Level Six behaviour is rubbing your breasts, while your Level Nine behaviour is rubbing your breasts and moaning. He'll realize that he has to stay in Level Six for longer, help you get up to Level Nine (where he has probably been since you rang him), then thrust away until you *both* get there.

Got me? It sounds far more complicated than it is. To master it, you'll just have to get down and dirty and see for yourselves. It is achievable, but more importantly, it's worth achieving.

'Telling each other Levels was embarrassing at first, but quickly became horny. Hearing him say he was at Level Eight made me get there too! When we came together, I cried. Very emotional.'

TRACEY, TWENTY-NINE

Multiple orgasms

I used to think that every other woman in the world had multiple orgasms, just like I used to think every other young girl had a pony. I know now both aren't true. (Unless the girls who had ponies grew up to have multiples... which is possible.) Truth is, every woman can have a multiple orgasm, but most of us don't.

Want one? Well, it's easier than writing a letter to Santa Claus. All you have to do is learn to master your PC or pelvic floor muscles. These are the muscles that contract when you come – you can sometimes feel them fluttering away inside you during an orgasm. Experts believe this happens so the muscles push the spermatozoids up the vagina into the cervix. And the stronger the muscles are, the more they contract, and the longer your orgasms can go on for. Plus, these muscles are rich in nerve endings, so the feelings you get when they kick-off inside you... Bliss.

Master your muscles

I want you to start by finding your PC muscles. How?
Squeeze up inside yourself, as if you wanted to stop
yourself weeing. Feel that muscle working? It's your PC
muscle. And we're going to work it out by squeezing and
releasing it as hard and quickly as possible, twenty times.

That's how Kegel exercises go, invented in the 1950s
by Dr Kegel, to help women's wombs to recover after
childbirth. They work wonders today – it's really just a
question of remembering to do twenty sets of rapid
squeezes every day.

Once you've isolated the muscles, you can also try the
gentler, more Pilates-style workout. Clench and release
your PC muscles in time with your breathing, slowly, for
about three minutes. They will start tingling, which
shows the blood is flowing into them.

TOOL BOX

*Vaginal exercisers are available from sex shops everywhere.
The best kind are weighted plastic balls that you insert into
the vagina.*

Go multiple

Once you have these bionic-strength muscles, you have to use them. How? Here's the drill. During sex, use those muscles to clench and release on his penis. This will send the blood flowing down into your vagina. When you feel your first orgasm approaching, I want you to stop it. Why? Because it's the final release of blood from your PC muscles that causes the blissful contractions. So the longer you delay that release, the bigger your climax will finally be.

So, as your orgasm approaches, ask your man to stop moving. He stays inside you until the tingly sensations die off. Then he starts moving again, and you start clenching and releasing again. You should soon feel the orgasm trying to happen again. Should you let it? Uh-uh. Have him stop again until it fades. Then one last final shag. This time, when you feel those pre-orgasmic sensations, keep clenching your PC muscles as hard as possible. Clench and release! As you do, your orgasmic contractions will start to kick in, and because you've delayed it, your orgasm will just go on and on.

That's the first technique. It gives you one super-long orgasm, which is caused by your powerful PC contractions and delayed gratification. There's another way. Start shagging again – but this time, when you feel the orgasm approaching, don't stop. Go with it. And tell your man to keep going too – no speeding-up, no stopping, he keeps doing exactly what he was. (But he's not allowed to come yet.) After your orgasm, just keep going. Even if you feel a little over-sensitive down there, keep shagging. This steady, repeated sex is just what you need to help another orgasm arrive. It will take longer – maybe another five to ten minutes. But keep at it, and you will come again.

With those super-powered PCs, your orgasms will be bigger, stronger and longer. And with your clenching control, you'll be able to dick-tate whether you have one toe-curling loooooong orgasm, or loads of little ones.

And him!

Yep, it's not *all* just you, you, you. Men can have multiples too. Tell him so, next time you forget his birthday. The trick is the same: he has to learn to control his PC muscles. When he can, it'll help him separate the feelings of climax with the feelings of ejaculating.

Anal sex

Just thinking about this is enough to scare the, er, shit out of most women. And rightly so – anal sex can hurt if it's done roughly or you're not prepared. But if you are... 'I loved anal sex with my boyfriend. Somehow it feels dirtier and kinkier than any other kind of shag. I'm lucky that his penis is long and not incredibly wide, so it doesn't hurt. With my ex it would have felt like giving birth in reverse,' Sandra, twenty-one.

I'm with Sandra on this. It *does* feel dirty, in an 'I'm a wild sex goddess and I'll do anything to get off' sort of way. It's a completely different sensation to normal sex and one that, eventually, you can learn to love as much as your partner does. It might even end up that *you're* the one pestering *him* to do it up your bum, instead of his nagging you every Christmas morning.

Don't try it doggy-style on the first time. Instead, lie on your side, with your back to your (stunned and not-quite-believing-his-luck) boyfriend. Get plenty of lubrication in. He squeezes lots on his fingertips then gently starts rubbing your bottom-hole with one finger. Smooth, swirly strokes around the hole feel great, and aren't scary. When *you* say so, he inserts that finger into your bum, up to about the first knuckle. Unless he's got fingers the size of bananas, you should be enjoying that. Soon he can insert another finger in, up to that knuckle. Then here's the clever bit: He pours lubricant down those two fingers so it goes inside you. Soon you'll feel like you want more stimulation, so he can push both fingers in a bit deeper.

Then, it's penis time. He should wear a condom, always. Anal sex can spread infections, so he has to go in wrapped. With lots of lubrication, he can insert just the very tip of his penis into your bottom. Then he has to *stop* and just hold it in place. *No thrusting*! At first, you'll feel incredibly filled-up, and you'll tense your muscles in panic. If he pushed it all the way in then, it'd be agony. So he holds it there until your panic fades. *It will.*

When you feel ready for more, you can push backwards onto his penis, taking him in at your own pace. You can reach around and grasp his shaft while you go, so you can feel how deeply he has gone in. When you've taken all you can, he can start shagging your bottom gently. You'll soon feel like you need more vaginal stimulation, so rub your clitoris, and use your fingers to fill yourself up.

Panic attacks!

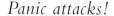 **Will there be poo?**
It's unlikely. Honestly. I know you feel like your
bottom is one big bag of plop, but it is actually
all stored way, way up inside where no man
could reach. If you're worried, have him take
the condom off in the dark.

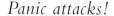 **Will it damage me?**
Not if it's done carefully. This is where his slow
speed and gentleness are vital! Too hard
thrusting might weaken the sphincter muscles,
so tell him you're on a Go-Slow or it's No-Go.

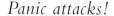 **Will there be, er, repercussions?**
Really want to know? OK then. Afterwards, or
the next day, you might possibly find
that your bottom is sore, or
that your, er, control is
slightly lessened. But that'll
soon pass.

Tantric sex

It's amazing how many people are unaware of the ins and outs of Tantric sex. Everyone has heard of this ancient Eastern art, but the definitions from the layman are hopelessly vague. 'That's the one where you lie there and do nothing, yeah?' asked my ex, 'because in that case, I learnt everything from you.'

The truth is that Tantric sex is a way of making sex last for ever. Really. It combines the mystical arts of meditation and spirituality with the staying power of an elastic band round your boyfriend's nuts. Even its name is promising – from the Indian *tantra*, it translates as 'expanded tool', which explains why the lady in my local curry house always looks so chipper. So here is an introduction to Tantric sex you can try at home with your lover.

Meet lingam and yoni

Like foreigners, Tantric sex has different names for things that you must master. Yoni refers to your front-bottom; lingam is your man's manhood. As Tantric sex is all about the mystical connection between these two energy forces, you must first get to know them. So, one quiet evening, both you and your partner strip naked and relax on the bed. Taking turns, you gently stroke and look at each other's bits without trying to arouse your partner at all. You just get to know them and develop a spiritual rapport.

Synchronize breathing

Breathing is big in Tantric sex. They recommend you do it throughout your sessions and, in fact, your life. Both lie on the bed on your left sides, in the spoons position (him behind you). Without thinking of anything, listen closely to each others' breathing. The man (or shiva) should try to synchronise his breathing to that of the woman (shikati). Inhale for four seconds, hold for four seconds, exhale for four seconds then pause for four seconds. When your breathing is matched, try this simple visualization exercise: imagine your breath is coming in through your yoni and being expelled through your mouth. He imagines his breath is coming in through his mouth and being expelled through his lingam. This connects your chakras (the spot in-between your eyebrows) and creates a powerful circle of energy between the two of you. (Or, if you're even slightly tired, makes you lose consciousness.) When you are spiritually joined in this way, turn

towards each other and look into each others' third
eyes (chakras) for five minutes, to create a bond.

Get on an Eastern promise

Sit in the yab-yom position (you on top, facing your
partner, your legs wrapped round his back). Gently
introduce lingam to yoni. Introduce it as deeply as
possible, then just – do nothing. Gaze into each others'
third eyes, and synchronize your breathing. Keep still,
and both flex your PC muscles. Against all
expectations, you'll begin to feel yourself reaching a
point of intense pleasure. Relax into it, and you'll
reach a higher one. And so on. Eventually you'll feel
ecstasy such as you've never felt before.

TRY THIS NOW!

*While in the yab-yom position, softly massage your lover's
perineum and the soft spot between his coccyx and anus in
circular motions eighty-one times. (This is a mystical Eastern
number.) It will release all his stored-up energy into his
system and he'll feel brilliant.*

OOPS! WHAT WENT WRONG?

This is the chapter you can turn to when good shags go bad. All your orgasmic problems are answered, and with a little grace, patience and intuition, 'screwing' should no longer be accompanied by the word 'up'.

7

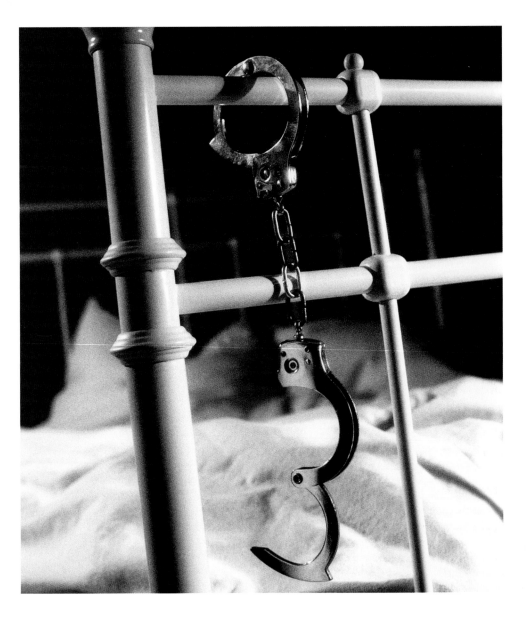

Bondage

'Is bondage dangerous?'

No. Scared? Remember the three S's: Do it
with a *steady* partner; use *silky* ties (easier
to untie); have a *safe* word to scream out when
it gets intense. Establish it beforehand: When
you scream, 'RED!' he stops. That way you can
still get off on saying, 'Untie me, you barbarian!'

Concentration

**'I can't concentrate when my lover goes down on me! I
feel so stupid. My mind just fills up with other stuff,
and I can't orgasm or even relax. HELP!'**

This used to happen to me. The trick is to keep
focusing on what he's doing! Don't let your mind
wander off unless it is going into your favourite
fantasy. Instead, hold his head with your hands (this
focuses you).

Then concentrate on the delicious sensations his
tongue and lips are creating. Feel everything – and keep
your breathing slow and steady. It'll take time, but
you'll soon be able to stay with the action.

Bored

'I'm bored with sex, so I rarely come.'
The next chapter is for you so keep reading and you'll learn how to keep it interesting. Or have fun with the 'try this now!' tips.

Aids

'I've never had an AIDS test. My partner won't sleep with me until I do.'
Get one. The easiest, least traumatic way of getting an AIDS test is to donate blood. They'll test it for AIDS, hepatitis, anaemia – everything. If there's anything wrong, they'll contact you. Also, some insurance companies will not cover you if you've had an official, hospital or clinic AIDS test – they think you're at risk. Besides, you get biscuits when you give blood.

Body-image

'I always want to shag in darkness, as I hate my body.'
To men, there is no such thing as an ugly woman, naked in bed, wanting to have sex. Use candlelight – so flattering. And keep some clothes on – a silky negligée will show off your boobs but hide your tummy.

Contraception

'What form of contraception would be best for me?'

Condoms

Works by: Stops his semen being released into your body.

How to use it: Slide it on before sex.

Effectiveness: Almost 99 per cent if put on *before* you start shagging. Putting it on halfway through is way risky.

Good for: You, if he's a new partner and you want protection against AIDS and STDs; and you can experiment with ribbed and studded ones.

Bad for: You, if he's so big it is likely to split; you're impulsive and given to, 'Oh just shove it in' urges; you hate the feel of them.

Get them: Free at Family Planning Clinics (FPCs). Or at chemists.

The Pill – Mini Pill, Combined Pill

Works by: Raising your levels of oestrogen and progesterone hormones, as happens naturally during pregnancy. Your body thinks it's pregnant, so it stops producing eggs to be fertilized, and creates a mucus 'plug' over the cervix. Nice.

How to use it: Take it every day.

Effectiveness: About 99 per cent.

Good for: You, if you hate having periods (the Pill stops them, or lightens them); you're in a steady relationship (it won't stop AIDS or STDs); you aren't liable to forget to take them.

Bad for: You, if you're over thirty-five or you smoke; you're too scatty to remember to take them regularly; you're sleeping with lots of partners.

Get them: Free at FPCs or from your doctor.

Morning After Pill

Works by: Giving your body oestrogen and progesterone. This either stops your body from ovulating, or stops a fertilized egg implanting in the womb (depending when in your cycle you took it).

How to use it: Take it up to seventy-two hours after unprotected sex. Two pills, twelve hours apart.

Effectiveness: 95 per cent if taken within the time-limit.

Good for: The very occasional accident.

Bad for: Regular use. This is *emergency* contraception. The hormone dosage is massive, so you don't want to take it regularly – your breasts will fall off! Plus it can make you feel nauseous.

Get them: Free at FPCs or through your doctor, or you can now buy it from some chemists.

Cunnilingus

'My boyfriend is mad keen to go down on me, but it does nothing for me and I find it embarrassing.'
It's not unusual to have oral disappointments. It is a *very* intimate act, and any insecurities you might be feeling could stop you relaxing and enjoying it. Or maybe your past lovers were not so hot down there. Show your man Chapter three of this book. Then, after a long bath, fling yourself on the bed and tell him to try his best. Still nothing? Then encourage him to grow a goatee. I'm serious. It'll tickle your fancy a treat.

Did he enjoy it?

'How do I know if my boyfriend really enjoys sex with me? Asking, "How was it for you?" is embarrassing.'
I know how you feel. The simple answer is, if he's shagging you regularly, he enjoys it. Men never do *anything* they don't want to. Also, he might be a bit shy of raving about the sex in case he thinks you don't like it much. Next time, tell him how brilliant it was, and use specific details – 'I loved the way you kissed me when I came', for example. That should open him up to returning the compliments.

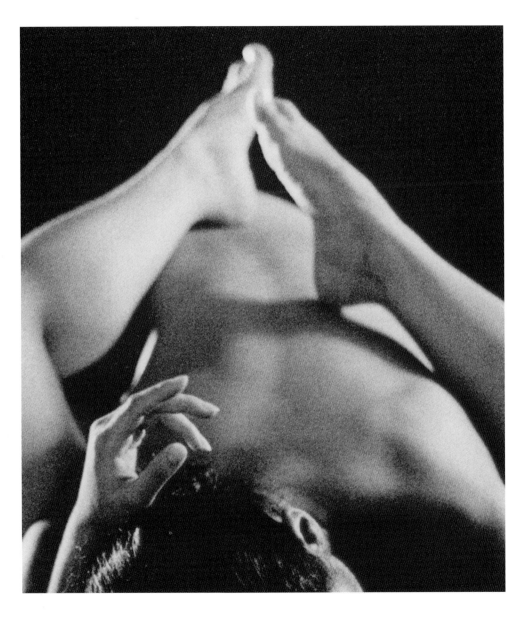

Three's a crowd?

'My man keeps asking me if I want to bring my
girlfriend home for the night. Should I?'

If you feel its something that takes your fancy, why
not give it a whirl. But do it for you, not for him.
And check out if she is interested first. That way you
can both surprise him when he least suspects it. And
no, it doesn't automatically make you a lesbian.

Gymnastic sex

'My man always wants us to change positions about ten times per shag. Am I wrong to be distracted by such gymnastic sex?'

No. In fact, he's showing off. Women need slow, sustained stimulation to come. So explain that you will orgasm more easily if you shag in just one position. Then try a sexy shag, you on top, and masturbate yourself until you come. When he sees how sexy one position can be, and how much you like it, he'll relax and stop trying to impress you with his moves.

Did she enjoy it?

'I'm worried my girlfriend isn't totally satisfied with our sex life.'

Why? Have you caught her in bed with a rolling-pin and a blow up Alsatian? If not, you could be worrying about nothing. Give her lots of attention and compliments, and she will feel sexy and special and 'safe' enough to return them. Plus, she'll get better in bed: women need to feel appreciated before they do exciting things like tango into the bedroom dressed in bubblewrap.

Masturbation

'My boyfriend is suspicious of me because I
masturbate regularly. Should I stop?'

Yup – stop seeing him. Who is he, the Vagina Police?
Your body is *your* body. Enjoy it. You could try
explaining to him, gently and soothingly, that just
because you masturbate, doesn't mean you're not
satisfied with him. Or just knock him unconscious
with your vibrator and enjoy the peace.

Nose-breaking

'When my lover gives me oral sex, I buck my hips
wildly as I come. He says it's going to break his nose!
How do I stop?'

Are you sitting on top of him? I guess so. So... try this
position. You kneel on all-fours, he slides up
underneath you, facing upwards, and does it like that.
(Lets hope he doesn't sneeze, though.)

Premature ejaculation

'My partner suffers from premature ejaculation. Any ideas?'

Use him as an egg timer? No? Then try this killer trick: when he's about to come, grasp the base of his penis firmly in your hand and squeeze – not so hard that his eyes bulge, but quite hard. It will stop the flow of semen from his testicles and buy you some more time. With practise, this will also boost his confidence ('I'm no longer Mr Ten Seconds!') and he'll get better by himself.

Sex-drives

'My boyfriend and I have completely different sex
drives. Help us!'

There's a simple cure for this. Talk about it and agree to
shag whenever the lesser-lusty partner wants to. But *they*
have to initiate it. The sex-crazed maniac half of the couple
isn't allowed to get huffy/grumpy/other people's phone
numbers if a night passes with no nookie going on.

Vaginismus

'I always seem to tense up when my boyfriend tries to
penetrate me. Could I have Vaginismus?'

It's unlikely. This is a psychological disorder that can
force the vagina muscles to clench tightly before sex, so
penetration is impossible.

Vibrators

'What are your recommendations for a "starter" vibrator?'

The important things about vibrators aren't length or
girth, they're speed and power. You'll use them mainly
for stimulating your clitoris, and not for actually
inserting. So choose a small, dainty one that packs a lot
of punch. You can even buy vibrators that fit into a
handbag – great for emergency stimulation.

Your long-term moans answered

'Why all this hard-work sex stuff?
Surely great sex should just happen...'
Oh please! Did driving just happen? Did walking just
happen? What makes you such a natural sex goddess
that you need no outside stimulus at all to keep your
lover interested? Sorry if that came out too angrily, but
it's true: sex takes research and effort. Do it. It is not a
sign of incompatibility when your sex life gets dull:
it's a sign of laziness. Don't change men; change
your sheets.

'He should make the effort to keep it
interesting if he loves me...'
He is making the effort, every time he tries to shag
you, every time he winks at you, every time he holds
your hand. That is a man making an effort. (He
doesn't do any of that? Book him a taxi, sweetie – one
way.) Men's egos are fragile, so they 'make an effort'
by obviously wanting *you*. They don't do it by trying
new stuff. It's your job to keep sexy and tempting
enough to keep them coming back for more.

'I feel too ugly to bother...'
Are you ugly? Genuinely? Do babies cry when you
pass? Then *change it*. Not for him, but because you
have to as a *female*. It's our equivalent of kicking
someone for spilling our pint. We need to feel
attractive. Do it for you. And everyone else on the bus.

'He's too ugly for me to bother with...'
Hmmm. Tougher, but fixable. Recall what first
attracted you. Hopefully it's his eyes, or smile –
something that gaining weight while losing hair won't
have hidden. Keep notes of how you feel about him
every day. Good things will emerge – use them to
motivate you to shave your legs and hide a dirty
G-string under his pillow. Ask him to write you a list
of ten things that are sexy about you. He might not be
ugly at all – you might be harbouring resentments and
feelings of low self-esteem. Nuke 'em.

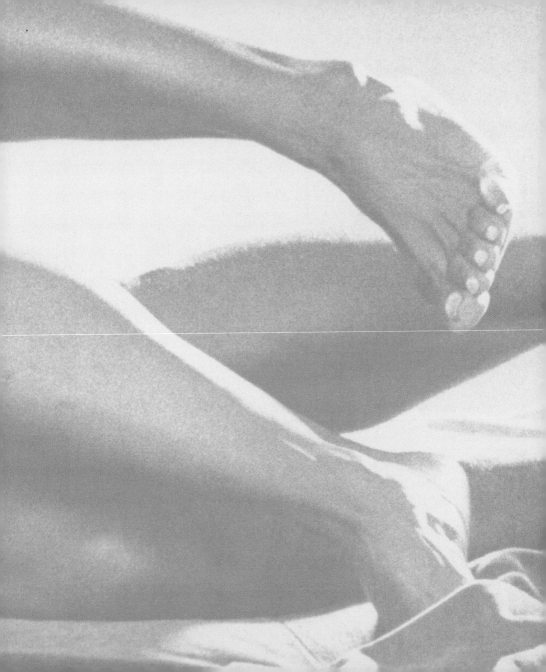

KEEPING
IT REAL
GOOD

This is the final stage of your Orgasm Education. Hopefully by now you've discovered how to have the biggest, best and wildest orgasms of your life. Good for you! Long may they continue. And they will, if you follow the advice – most of it from orgasmically successful long-term couples – here.

8

Keeping it hot and spicy

The most important trick is to keep the excitement levels up. That's why you orgasm, after all – it's the blissful moment when that excitement reaches its climax. Keep that in mind, and it's easy to see that months of staying in at nights, wearing matching pyjamas and watching videos will not keep you orgasmically satisfied. Try to balance the intimacy of a long-term relationship with the mystery and passion of a fling, and you should reap the rewards of both.

Why it gets dull

So many reasons. The excitement goes, you stop making an effort, you use the gym only for its chocolate machines... You know why sex gets dull. The trick is to find the motivation to *change it*. Here are the most common sexual bores:

- ❀ No effort is made anymore
- ❀ Too busy with domestic chores
- ❀ Same bodies
- ❀ No surprises
- ❀ No 'Will they like me?' active interest
- ❀ Routines get set and are hard to break

So here's what to do

How can I advise you on long-term sex? Good question. I'm so commitment-phobic I can't even get long books out of the library. So, instead, I asked the happiest couples I know for their advice. Here it is.

Sweet not-no-nothings

'Daniel and I have always called each other affectionate names like "gorgeous" and "sexy" and "beautiful". It doesn't sound much, but it keeps us feeling sexy and desirable to each other. Which keeps us shagging!'

PAULA, TWENTY-THREE

Don't rely on him to make you feel sexy

'Sexiness comes from within. So I make sure I keep doing things that make me feel like a sexy woman – exercising, getting manicures, buying new clothes. That way, I never have to question why Mark wants to have sex with me. I know I'm sexy! Why wouldn't he? It keeps my self-confidence high, which boosts my libido.'

MATILDA, TWENTY-FIVE

Read one sex book a year

'It started as a joke, but Matthew and I now buy each other a sex book every year on the anniversary of our first shag. Just reading them gets us going, as does our ritual: we turn to page 79 and do whatever it says on it first. We act out the picture, or try the technique. That's seen us do doggie anal, new blowjobs, dressing up... Fun, and sexy.'

RINTJE, THIRTY

Final tips for you and him...
to try tonight

❀ Be waiting naked when he comes home.

❀ Rent a porn film and learn the plot. Then put the film on for your man and tempt him to a real-life reenactment.

❀ Try the Tantric Thrust Technique: during sex, have him make nine short, sharp thrusts, then three long, slow, deep ones. Repeat as necessary.

❀ Snog him for thirty minutes – no groping allowed.

❀ Get naked and feed seafood to each other.

❀ Ask him to shave off all your pubic hair, then pour Champagne over your clitoris. Bubbles galore.

Happy humping darlings!

Publisher Silvia Langford

Editorial Director Toria Leitch

Designer Mark Latter

Printed and bound in Vicenza, Italy